Energy in Action™

WATER POWER

The Rosen Publishing Group's
PowerKids Press™
New York

Ian F. Mahaney

Published in 2007 by The Rosen Publishing Group, Inc.
29 East 21st Street, New York, NY 10010

First Edition

Editor: Joanne Randolph
Book Design: Julio Gil

Photo Credits: Cover, title page © Roger Wood/Corbis; p. 4 © Photodisc; p. 5 © www.istockphoto.com/James Boulette; p. 6 © www.istockphoto.com/Matthew Cole; p. 7 © www.istockphoto.com/Doug Webb; p. 8 © www.istockphoto.com/Amanda Rohde; p. 9 © www.istockphoto.com/Rick Jones; p. 11 © www.istockphoto.com/Jason Cheever; p. 12 Erich Lessing/Art Resource, NY; p. 13 © Warren Faidley/Corbis; p. 15 © Bettmann/Corbis; p. 16 © www.istockphoto.com/Kevin Bergen; p. 17 © Attar Maher/Corbis Sygma; p. 18 © www.istockphoto.com/Meredith Lamb; p. 19 © www.istockphoto.com/Malcolm Romain; p. 21 Adriana Skura; p. 22 Cindy Reiman.

Library of Congress Cataloging-in-Publication Data

Mahaney, Ian F.
   Water power / Ian F. Mahaney.— 1st ed.
      p. cm. — (Energy in action)
   Includes index.
   ISBN (10) 1-4042-3481-0 (13) 978-1-4042-3481-9 (lib. bdg.) —
ISBN (10) 1-4042-2190-5 (13) 978-1-4042-2190-1 (pbk.)
   1. Water-power—Juvenile literature. I. Title. II. Series: Energy in action (PowerKids Press) III. Series.
TC146.M34 2007
333.91'4—dc22

                                    2005035825

Manufactured in the United States of America

CONTENTS

Water and Its States

Water covers 70 **percent** of Earth's surface. We find about 97 percent of water in Earth's oceans. The rest can be found underground and in lakes and rivers. Most water we see on Earth is a liquid, but water can be a solid and a gas, too. Have you ever seen a frozen lake? Water becomes solid ice when **temperatures** fall below 32° **Fahrenheit** (0° **Celsius**). Water becomes a gas at 212° F (100° C). If you boil a pot of water, steam rises above the water. This is water in a gas form.

Water is very powerful. People have learned to use the power in water for things like creating electricity.

4

Opposite: This view of Earth from space shows how much of Earth is covered by water. Everything that is blue is the ocean. *Above:* These young people enjoy water in its solid form as they skate on a frozen pond.

Gravity

You have surely noticed that when you jump into the air, you fall back to Earth. The force that makes this happen is called **gravity**. Gravity acts much like a large bar magnet. A bar magnet **attracts** metal scraps, such as paper clips. In the same way, gravity on Earth pulls all objects toward the center of Earth. When you ride your bike down a hill, do you notice that you do not need to pedal? This is because gravity is taking you and your bike to a place that is closer to the center of Earth. Gravity has an effect on everything on Earth, including water. It provides water with much of its power.

Opposite: This magnet has attracted paper clips to itself. *Above:* These racers depend on gravity as they dive off the racing blocks. They know that as they jump off into the air, they will move down and hit the water.

Speed and Movement of Water

Did you know that all rivers and streams flow downhill? This is gravity at work. The Hudson River in New York is an excellent example. The Hudson begins in the Adirondack Mountains in northern New York State. It flows downhill from areas of great **elevation** to those of lower elevation. Elevation is the height of land above **sea level**. Sea level is the height of the top of the ocean. Rivers and streams flow from areas of higher elevation to areas of lower elevation, because gravity pulls the water downward. Water in most rivers will at some point reach sea level and join the oceans. The movement of water creates a lot of **energy**, or the power to do work.

Opposite: This is the mouth of a river. The mouth is the place where the river and its streams empty into the ocean. *Above:* This river begins in the Mendocino mountain range in California and flows downhill to the Pacific Ocean.

What Can Water Accomplish?

Water is very powerful. It has energy that is able to accomplish great tasks on Earth. Rushing water can create giant cuts in Earth. An example is the Grand Canyon in northern Arizona. The Grand Canyon is a huge **gorge** in Earth's surface. At the bottom of the canyon runs the Colorado River. It might seem unbelievable, but the Colorado River created the Grand Canyon. Over millions of years, the strong river wore away the surrounding rock, lowering the elevation of the river. Today the Colorado River flows more than 1 mile (1.6 km) below the surface of the Grand Canyon. Water is very powerful indeed!

The Colorado River cuts a path through the Grand Canyon. The river's continuous motion against the rocks has worn them down over a long time. The water then carries away the rock it has broken down. This is called weathering and erosion.

Controlling Water

Sometimes so much water is trying to rush downhill that there is more water than the riverbanks can handle. When this happens floods occur. Floods can be beneficial or harmful to an area. Floods overrun the riverbanks, which can **irrigate** nearby farmland, helping crops grow. On the other hand, floodwaters flowing through homes and businesses can destroy property and make an area unlivable. People have learned to control rivers and floods by building dams. Dams built in rivers keep the river from following its natural path. Stopping the water creates large **reservoirs** of water that build up behind the dam. We can let this water out when we need it.

Opposite: In 1902, the island of Philae, shown here, was flooded as the Old Aswan Dam in Egypt stopped the flow of the river. The waters of the river collected and covered the island with water. *Above:* This town in Alabama was flooded when a powerful storm called a hurricane hit.

Water for Electricity

Dams are used for more than just holding back water. When the water stored behind a dam is let out, it has the power to do important work. We use this water power to make electricity. Electricity is energy that we use every day to make our lives comfortable and productive.

The Grand Coulee Dam is one of the largest dams in the United States. This dam produces the most electricity in the United States. Like other dams, the Grand Coulee Dam creates electricity by forcing water through turbines, which are like large fans. The turbine is forced to spin quickly by the water rushing through it. The movement of the turbine is used to create electricity in a power station housed near the dam.

The Grand Coulee Dam is the largest producer of electricity created by water in the United States. The dam also provides the water for 500,000 acres (202,343 ha) of farmland.

The Oceans

The water in rivers and streams makes up only a small part of Earth's water supply. Most of Earth's water is in the oceans. This water is always on the move. Ocean currents cause the water to continuously move to different areas of Earth. The ocean also moves higher or lower. This is called a tide.

The power of the ocean could be a huge **source** of electricity if we created the **technology** to use it. We have already created technologies that allow us to use a small amount of the ocean's power. For example, France successfully makes some of its electricity from tides today.

Opposite: If you have ever spent time near the ocean, you may have noticed that the ocean waves reach different points on the beach during the day. This is the tide moving in and out.
Above: France's one power station, in La Rance, gets its power from the tide. When the tide rushes in or out, the water spins a turbine. This creates electricity.

Renewable Energy

Most of the electricity we use today comes from **fuels** we call **nonrenewable resources**. Coal and oil are examples of nonrenewable sources of energy. Water power is a **renewable** resource. This is an advantage that water power has over nonrenewable resources. We can run the same water through a turbine over and over again. Water power is also clean energy. Nonrenewable sources, like coal, put dirt and gases into the air when we use them to make power. This hurts our **environment**. Finding better ways to use water power is one way we can make affordable power without harming nature.

Opposite: This is one of the towers that takes in water at the Hoover Dam in Nevada. Water is a renewable and clean energy source. *Above:* Coal is being mined here. Once the coal has been mined completely, there will be no coal left in this area.

Experiments with Water: Putting Gravity to Work

SUPPLIES NEEDED:

plastic soda or juice bottle, a cork, scissors, large nail, toothpicks, clay, rubber tubing, funnel, tape, sheet of stiff plastic, a bowl, colored water

As you have learned, the force of gravity gives water much of its power. Gravity will push water over a mountain to create a waterfall. A large waterfall can pour over a huge waterwheel in a power station to create electricity. This experiment shows how a waterwheel works.

Step 1 Have an adult cut off the bottom of a plastic soda or juice bottle. Then ask an adult to make holes in opposite sides of the bottle with a large nail.

Step 2 Next make the paddles for your waterwheel. Cut a sheet of stiff plastic into four pieces that are ½ by 2½ inches (1.3 by 6.4 cm). Cut four evenly spaced openings in a cork. Put the plastic pieces into the openings.

Step 3 Push a toothpick in one end of the cork. Holding the wheel sideways, place the cork into the bottle so that the toothpick fits through one hole. Push a toothpick into the other end of the cork.

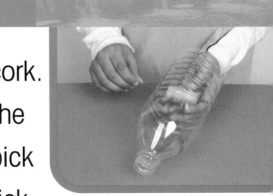

Step 4 Put clay at the ends of each toothpick for balance. Stand the bottle up in a bowl. Use strong tape to secure one end of the rubber tubing to the bottom of a funnel. Tape the other end of the tubing to the mouth of the bottle.

Step 5 Holding the funnel high, pour colored water into the funnel and the tubing. Watch gravity power your waterwheel.

Experiments with Water: Strong Liquids

A moving liquid can be a powerful force that is able to change the land in its path. For example, the water flowing in rivers or waterfalls can wear down solid rock over time. This experiment will show you how moving liquids can create change.

Step 1 Use rocks and soil in a shallow pan to make a model of a hill. Fill a pitcher or watering can with water.

Step 2 Pour the water over your hill. What happens? The force of the water moving over the rocks and soil changes the shape of your hill. When water moves over rocks or soil, it causes erosion. Erosion can change the shape of mountains.

Glossary

attracts (uh-TRAKTS) Pulls toward.

Celsius (SEL-see-us) A scale that measures the freezing point of water as 0° and the boiling point as 100°.

elevation (eh-luh-VAY-shun) The height of an object.

energy (EH-nur-jee) The power to work or to act.

environment (en-VY-ern-ment) Nature, or a person's or animal's surroundings.

Fahrenheit (FEHR-un-hyt) A scale that measures the freezing point of water as 32° and the boiling point as 212°.

fuels (FYOOLZ) Things used to make energy, warmth, or power.

gorge (GORJ) A steep, narrow passage through land.

gravity (GRA-vih-tee) The natural force that causes objects to move toward the center of Earth.

irrigate (IR-uh-gayt) To supply land with water through ditches or pipes.

nonrenewable (non-ree-NOO-uh-bul) Not able to be replaced once used.

percent (pur-SENT) One part of 100.

renewable (ree-NOO-uh-bul) Able to be replaced.

reservoirs (REH-zuh-vwarz) Stored bodies of water.

resources (REE-sors-ez) Supplies or sources of energy or useful things.

sea level (SEE LEH-vul) The height of the top of the ocean.

source (SORS) A place from which something starts.

technology (tek-NAH-luh-jee) The way that people do something using tools, and the tools that they use.

temperatures (TEM-pur-cherz) How hot or cold things are.

Index

D

dam(s), 12, 14

E

electricity, 4, 14, 16, 18, 20
elevation, 8, 10
energy, 8, 10, 14, 18
environment, 18
erosion, 22

F

floods, 12

G

gorge, 10
gravity, 6, 8, 20–21

N

nonrenewable resources, 18

R

renewable resource, 18
reservoirs, 12

S

sea level, 8

T

technology, 16
temperatures, 4
tide(s), 16

Web Sites

Due to the changing nature of Internet links, PowerKids Press has developed an online list of Web sites related to the subject of this book. This site is updated regularly. Please use this link to access the list:
www.powerkidslinks.com/eic/water/